the
paper
florist

create and display
stunning paper flowers

the
paper
florist

suzi mclaughlin

photography by anna batchelor

Kyle Books

for Isla & Ava

contents

my life with paper

I am a passionate collector of stationery. Handmade papers, beautiful notebooks, vintage staplers, gold paperclips and translucent envelopes – these are the things that give me butterflies, that make my heart flutter with excitement.

My love affair with paper started when I was a child. I was amazed at all the things you could create with it; from cutting out snowflakes with stubby, plastic yellow-handled scissors, to gluing strips of brightly coloured sugar paper together to make chains to decorate our school hall at Christmas time, and making row upon row of paper dolls to colour in and animate. So many possibilities and all so easily accessible – I became a voracious little collector, squirrelling away scraps and strips from discarded newspapers and old magazines. I could always find paper around the house to fold, cut and pleat into something beautiful; a process that would keep me quietly entertained for hours. My fascination with paper continued into college and then later at university – when most other people had left playing with paper as a childhood pastime, I continued to cut, paste and fold.

My mother is from Mizoram, a remote region on the north-eastern border of India, bounded by Burma to the east and south and Bangladesh to the west. Growing up in Mizoram, crafting was an essential part of my mother's childhood, due in part to her remote location which meant imported materials were hard to come by. They had to be inventive and make use of what was available locally. Traditional Lungis (brightly coloured and patterned fabrics similar in style to a sari) were intricately handwoven, and bowls and plates were crafted from strips of bamboo tightly intertwined. For the last 25 years, my auntie, who still lives there, has made paper flowers for celebrations and for funerals. She uses the most basic materials,

with bamboo strips as stems and hand-cutting paper petals which she forms into blooms and secures with cotton thread. She only started using a glue gun five years ago! Her daughter helps her now, but before that, my mum and my Auntie Maggie would sit and spend many contented hours curling tiny individual paper petals. Even though I only found out about this 'family tradition' in the last few years, I like to think it's in my blood.

I fed my passion for stationery at university where I studied Textile Design; I would make sketchbooks from found papers, stitching them together and relishing the different textures and thickness of papers. For my coursework, I'd make all of my samples and prototypes out of paper first, but I'd always end up preferring them to my finished fabric pieces! This led to deciding for my final end of year degree show that I would abandon textiles completely and instead create a garden installation made entirely out of brightly coloured papers. I deconstructed real flowers so that I could reconstruct them in paper and used silhouettes of foliage to make paper garlands. The piece received lots of interest and over the following months commissions for my work began to flood in.

Now I work as a paper artist making paper flowers and plants for display, events and for exhibitions from my studio in rural Northamptonshire, where I can enjoy the peace and quiet of the rolling hills and beautiful woodland that I am lucky enough to have on my doorstep. I can often be found traipsing through the local woods and fields looking for inspiration in the surrounding flora and fauna, often with my mad labrador Huey in tow, and my young daughter, Ava, and fiancé, Steve, for company.

I like to think that I'm bringing paper flowers to a wider audience. I've created installations and bespoke items for leading brands and editorials such as Harvey Nichols, Harrods, John Lewis, Estée Lauder and ELLE magazine as well as window displays for Jo Malone London's flagship store. My life-sized paper garden, commissioned by the Royal Horticultural Society for BBC Gardeners' World Live Show, was even awarded an RHS gold medal!

Plants and flowers constantly inspire and inform my work; I am not a trained florist, I just have a huge appreciation for the natural world and an obsession with all things paper. I have really enjoyed making this book and I hope you will love it as much as I do!

Suzi

the wonderful world of paper flowers

Paper flowers can be used to create beautiful, original items for your home, friends and family that will look wonderful and last a lot longer than the real thing! You can make unique centrepieces, handmade presents and decorative one-off bouquets; all using methods and techniques demonstrated in this book.

Through *The Paper Florist* I hope to inspire you to make fun and original creations, helping you to transform a flat sheet of paper into something beautiful and unique. I have chosen to use a variety of papers for the flowers in this book, including the beautiful Colorplan papers from the James Cropper Paper Mill, which is the last existing, functioning paper mill here in the UK, as well as 'found' paper such as old letters, the pages of second-hand books and even old Ordnance Survey maps, which can all be repurposed into something new and beautiful. (See page 15 for more on paper types and weights.)

The aim is to give you the tools to make something precious from a very inexpensive and readily available material using just a few pieces of equipment. It's a much simpler crafting job than you might think, and step-by-step tutorials as to how to make paper petals and leaves, bouquets and even wreaths will make it even easier.

But first, let's look at where it all began.

the history of the paper flower

Soon after the invention of paper, in around 100 BC, the Chinese started fashioning it into flowers, which they would float in water as religious offerings. Bright and vibrant paper flowers have also featured in various ceremonies in Mexico for centuries, such as the Day of the Dead festival, weddings and other celebrations. They are often used in the place of real flowers as decorations for churches and homes. In England, Victorian women made them when real flowers were out of season to decorate their homes. It was a sign that you were a woman of means if you had the luxury of the time and resources needed to craft these blooms, which would be finished off by hand painting or dipping the petals in wax.

In recent years paper flowers have been enjoying a resurgence in popularity, with major fashion houses incorporating them into runway shows, retailers featuring floral arrangements in window displays and people choosing paper blooms for weddings. Bouquets, decorations and even buttonholes can be made in advance or at hen do craft parties, adding a lovely personal touch to a couple's special day. They can also easily be kept as a memento, handed down to future generations, without having to dry or preserve anything. Paper is also the symbol for first wedding anniversaries, making them a wonderful gift to mark the special occasion.

paper floristry

Paper flowers can come in any colour you like – the only limit is your imagination! Be adventurous with your creations; why not try colours that are not typically found in nature? Combine different-coloured petals and leaves with any stem or florist tape you like. If you're unsure about a combination, cut a small swatch of each colour and arrange them on a plain background to see if they will work well together.

Patterned paper can also be really effective, as can printed wrapping paper or marbled paper – a geometric or chevron pattern will give a really contemporary look. 'Found' papers are also a favourite of mine; old letters, maps and book pages are great, and even things that you might not have considered, such as old brown-paper bags, magazines or even notebook pages can make a beautiful flower. Use them either as the flower head, as leaves or the whole flower. You could use them for the stem, too; simply cut thin strips, wrap around florist wire and carefully secure with a glue gun.

Paper printed with messages can also make a unique, truly personal gift. Hand-written script or printed text could include names and dates or a message of your choice. If you go down the 'digital' route, repeat text down a page to fill the paper then print it, because once it is cut up only some words will be visible. Keep it short and sweet too, so that the message will be readable in full. Experiment with different fonts and letter size to see what works best and use any paper you like – just make sure you will be able to see the text when it takes its final form.

Just like the real thing, paper flowers can be used to make all kinds of arrangements. In this book I have shown a handful of ideas on how to use and display your blooms. Once you try these you will no doubt feel ready to give your own ideas a go, so experiment! Flowers can look great worn as a boutonniere for a wedding or tied around the wrist as a corsage. Create a bold display by hanging your stems from above or even attach the flowers and foliage directly to a wall to create an eye-catching installation. Your arrangements will not wilt and so can be enjoyed and reused repeatedly, or can be added to with new flowers at a later date to create a fresh new look.

The templates here will help you recreate the flowers in this book and are the same size as the flowers pictured. Simply photocopy the template onto some printer paper, glue the printout onto a piece of card and, once the glue has dried, cut out your shapes using a sharp pair of scissors. This will create a stiff template you can draw around onto your chosen paper. Alternatively, secure tracing paper over the template and draw around the shape using a sketching pencil, ensuring you press down hard to give a clear outline. Flip the tracing paper over onto some card (so the pencil side is face down), secure in place and, using your pencil, carefully scribble over the lines so it prints onto the paper underneath. Lift to check your progress as you go. Finally, remove the tracing paper and cut out the shapes using a sharp pair of scissors.

You may decide to experiment with the scale of the templates; you can scan them into your computer and reduce or increase the size when you go to print. To do this, select the scale option

within your print settings and reduce the size to 50% or increase it to 150%, if you like. View the template onscreen or print it onto cheap paper first to ensure it is the size you want, then keep playing until you have what you are looking for.

If you require much larger templates for oversized flowers, then it can be easier to take your scanned images into a copy shop or photocopy them directly out of the book to be printed onto A3 or A2 paper. Large versions of the flowers would make a great feature at a wedding or party, and mini versions are lovely as a gift – see the small bluebells on page 90.

The flowers here are a great starting point to get you going on your paper-flower making journey. Once you have some experience, why not get creative and use the templates to make you own inventions? Combine your choice of stamen with your favourite petals and leaves to create a hybrid. Bear in mind the size of the templates though; for instance, the peony centre would be too large for the hellebore petals, whereas the poppy centre would work proportionately with the peony petals. There are no rules, so let's get started.

choosing your paper

Once you've chosen a flower to make, the first thing to do is choose your materials. And, of course, paper is the priority. Below are a few pointers to bear in mind, as well as a few personal recommendations. You can get these papers from your local craft or stationery shops or have a browse online. See page 139 for a list of handy suppliers.

paper weight

Paper weight is measured in GSM (grams per square metre); the higher the number, the heavier the weight of the paper or the thicker it is. Standard printer paper is 80gsm (54lb), while thicker craft paper that I tend to use is between 135 and 160gsm (90 and 110lb).

paper grain

Just like wood, paper has a grain, because during the making process the fibres are all laid in one direction. When you fold a sheet in half, it bends more easily in one direction. This can be useful to know when using a bone folder (see page 20) to tear your paper, as the sheet will tear more easily with the grain, or leave a jagged edge against the grain.

You should also curl with the grain, so bear this in mind when cutting out individual petals. This might not always apply, because with a lot of the flowers the petals are not laid out in a row but joined in a circular shape or need curling in different directions, but it can be useful to know why the paper behaves the way it does.

coloured papers

GF Smith Colorplan Papers, manufactured at the James Cropper Paper Mill in the Lake District in the UK, are perfect for flowers; they make embossed papers in different textures which can look really great, especially for the leaves. I also love Daler Rowney's Murano pastel paper, as it has a naturally textured surface and high cotton content, which gives it a luxurious feel. At 160gsm (110lb) it makes beautiful yet durable flowers. Canford paper is another of my go-to materials of choice from the Daler Rowney range; it comes in 35 different colours and is great quality.

found papers

Found papers can be anything you can lay your hands on – old book pages, sheet music, maps or old letters can all be used. It's a great way to make your flowers really personal. Why not use pages from your favourite book, lyrics from a song you like or even your wedding vows for an anniversary gift?

There really are no limits – tracing paper, greaseproof paper, cupcake cases or even toilet paper can be transformed into flowers with a little experimentation.

It is more difficult to envisage the final outcome when using found papers, as you may not know the paper weight and how it will work. But half the fun of making is playing with papers and seeing how they can change the final look quite dramatically. The peony (page 104) looks great made from 135gsm (90lb) coloured paper, as pictured, but can also look beautiful when made with delicate tissue papers. Why not try making the same flower out of different paper types to see the difference, or combining two types of paper in one?

tools

You don't need many specialist tools for paper-flower making, some are essential, such scissors and a glue gun, and some will make it a whole lot easier. You might have a few at home already, and others are easily available from local craft shops or online.

scissors

A decent pair of sharp scissors is essential. It will make cutting out templates a lot easier and mean you can cut more than one sheet at once, which will speed up the process and move you on to the fun part sooner – the making! A small pair of scissors is useful for more intricate work such as small petals and delicate leaf shapes. It's best not to use fabric scissors, though, as paper will blunt them. A larger pair for cutting paper down to size and for the larger template shapes is also useful.

Whilst not what I would call an 'essential tool', I also love using small bonsai scissors. Not only are they beautiful to look at, they also have very sharp pointed blades which are great for cutting out very small flowers like the Jasmine (page 112). As they are super sharp and durable, unlike other scissors they can be used to cut florist wire, too, if you don't have your wire cutters to hand.

hot glue gun and glue sticks

You'll need this for all of the flowers in this book. Hot glue is strong once set and gives the flowers real durability. It also dries very quickly, allowing you to work at a fast pace. Do take care, though, as the melted glue can be very hot. Alternatively, a cool glue gun can be used, but I don't find they stick quite as well.

wooden skewer

I use a basic wooden skewer to curl the petals of most of my flowers. This simple object is the key to creating the 3-dimensional flower shapes you see in this book. A metal skewer or knitting needle could be used, but they can be more difficult as the paper can slip on the smooth surface. A cocktail stick is also great for curling very small petals or to create a tightly curled petal.

bone folder

Also called a folding bone, this is handy for any paper craft. The pointed tip pressed down onto folded edges gives a sharp crease, allowing you to tear it in a straight line. I also use this to curl flower petals as it's smoother than a scissor blade and leaves no marks. It can also score lines or make an impression; try replicating the veins on leaves.

pin or needle

Used to pierce a hole through the centre of the flowers or when wiring leaves. The end of a sharp scissor blade could be used if you require a larger hole.

white tack

When piercing a hole through paper this is placed underneath, allowing you to safely push a pin or needle through the paper to create a hole.

wire cutters

Used to cut the wire down to size. Don't use standard scissors for this as it will ruin them.

pliers

Generally used for shaping wire stems, especially on some of the smaller, more fiddly flowers. A basic pair of pliers is inexpensive and definitely a useful tool to have.

florist tape

This comes in a wide variety of colours; I have used green and brown in the book but any colour can be used depending on the colour scheme you are going for. The tape is self-adhesive and easy to use once you know how (see page 24). Used to cover wire stems, attach leaves, join stems together, or attach flowers to real tree branches. White tape is also great if you are making flowers out of book pages or other found papers. Keep the tape in an airtight container as it can dry out once opened.

florist wire

Wire comes in different gauges; the smaller the number, the thicker the wire. A 16-gauge wire is 1.63mm (0.06in) thick and ridged but still bendable, whereas a 30-gauge wire is

0.32mm (0.01in) thick, so soft and very flexible. Note that a 16-gauge wire in the UK is the equivalent to a 14-gauge wire in the US, 18-gauge equivalent to a 16-gauge wire and so on. But the difference in size is minimal, about 0.3mm. If you can't get hold of the exact size wire listed, it's fine to use the closest you can get. Any flexible wire can be used as it will be wrapped in florist tape anyway. Either cut to length as you go, or, if your wire is on a reel, cut the wire to the length you need before working with it.

paper clips

Handy if you are cutting multiple sheets of paper at a time as you can secure sheets together, depending on their thickness, before cutting. You could also use a stapler.

pencil and sharpener

It's important to ensure you use a sharp pencil when drawing around templates so you have a neat, clear-cut line and are able to draw between each flower petal.

craft knife

Use for scoring paper, such as with the Bluebell (page 90). It can also be used with a metal ruler on a cutting mat to cut paper down to size and to cut strips for stamens. I prefer using a craft knife for this over scissors as it gives a straighter line and can be quicker if you are cutting several pieces of paper.

metal ruler

A metal ruler is best for use with a craft knife on a cutting mat to score and cut paper to avoid splinters being chipped off a wooden ruler.

cutting mat

This will protect your surface when cutting or scoring with a craft knife. Most have a ruler and grid printed onto them, so they make measuring and cutting more precisely easy.

masking tape or washi tape

These can be used to temporarily stick your template down. Washi tape tends to be smaller so is great for small templates, while masking tape is good for larger templates and can be much cheaper. It can also be cut down for smaller shapes.

using florist tape

Florist tape is a wonderful material for crafting. As the name suggests, it is used by florists to bind together real flowers, but it works just the same with the paper variety and is incredibly versatile – you can use it to cover wire stems, to attach flowers or leaves to stems or to each other, to build up multiple blossoms (such as with Jasmine, page 112), or even attach two bits of wire together to extend the length of a stem if it's too short to display or style. The possibilities are endless, and once you know the basics of how it works, it's a fantastic tool. Begin practicing by wrapping simple single stems and you'll learn the technique in no time.

wrapping wire stems

1. Take your chosen florist tape and stretch it to expose its sticky adhesive. You will notice one side is stickier than the other – this is the side that will need to be in contact with the wire.

2. Place the wire onto the florist tape at an angle and tightly wrap it, pulling and stretching the tape as you go. This technique can take some practice; be patient, though, you might need to wrap several wires to get the hang of it, but once you do you will be surprised at how quickly you will be able to wrap stems!

3. Once you reach the bottom of the wire stem, twist the tape until it snaps off neatly.

attaching leaves and stems

you will need:

Florist tape • Small sharp scissors

1. Attaching leaves and stems to wire with florist tape is easy. Place the flower stems or leaf wires you wish to attach either together in a bunch or hold them in place along the stem if you want to attach them at different heights.

2. Stretch the florist tape to expose the sticky adhesive inside and begin to wrap around the stems, pulling the tape downwards and wrapping at an angle. Keep going either until you reach the end or add in more stems further down by placing them directly next to the existing stems, and continue to wrap them all together.

3. Once you reach the end of the stem, twist the florist tape until it breaks off neatly.

making flower stamen

In biological terms, the centre of a flower is called different things depending on the function it has; the pollen-bearing part is called the stamen, while the seed-bearing part is known as the pistil. For the purpose of clarity here I've referred to the central piece of each flower as the stamen throughout. Most can be represented using one of the three styles: a small bud, a large ball or a fringed roll. The first is used for delicate flowers, such as the Ranunculus (page 50), while the large ball is used for sturdier flowers such as the Poppy (page 56). Finally, the fringed centre can be made at any size for many different flowers, such as the Hellebore (page 62) or the Aster (page 76).

bud stamen

you will need:

Cotton bud • Small sharp scissors
24-gauge wire, or similar • Green florist
tape

1. Take a cotton bud and, using a sharp pair of scissors, cut
    the stick approximately 1cm (½in) down from the base of
    one of the cotton-wool tips. (Keep the other end of the bud
    if you are making more than one stamen.)

2. Insert the tip of a pair of small sharp scissors into the hollow
    plastic stick and very carefully twist to reopen the hole,
    which may have been squeezed closed during cutting.
    Push a 28–30cm long piece of the wire inside the plastic
    stick, then twist and push until it feels securely in place.

3. Pull off a little green florist tape from the roll to expose
    the sticky adhesive inside, then tape from the bottom of
    one side of the cotton-wool over the top to the other side,
    and pinch in place at the base of the bud with your fingers.
    Holding the tape in place, carefully wrap the rest of the
    stick in tape, smoothing it down as you go so you have a
    sleek finish and pulling it as you go so it adheres securely.
    Once all the plastic is wrapped, continue to wrap the tape
    all the way down the wire stem (see page 25).

ball stamen

you will need:

Green crepe or tissue paper to make a 1.5cm (¾in) ball • Hot glue gun and glue sticks • 20-gauge wire, or similar, 28–30cm (11–12in) long • 5cm (2in) square of green crepe paper • Small sharp scissors • Green florist tape

1. Take some crepe or tissue paper and roll into a ball approximately 1.5cm (¾in) in diameter.

   Apply some hot glue to the balled-up paper and stick a wire into the ball, pushing it firmly into the paper and holding it until the glue dries – you can add more glue later if it needs further reinforcement.

2. Stretch out the green crepe-paper square – it should be big enough to cover the paper ball. Place the ball into the centre of the crepe-paper square and wrap the paper around it, taking care to smooth it as you go and to trim any excess paper from around the bottom if it won't lie smoothly against the wire stem.

3. Wrap the stem in green florist tape, stretching the tape to expose the sticky adhesive within it. Start at the ball, wrapping as closely as you can to the ball centre over the top of the excess crepe paper, keeping it tight as you go. Continue down the wire stem (see page 25).

fringed stamen

you will need:

Paper • Florist wire • Small sharp scissors
Hot glue gun and glue sticks

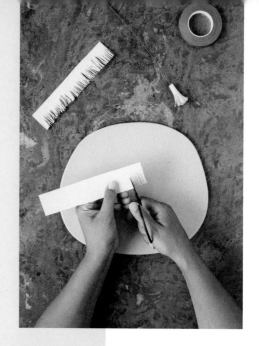

1. Cut out the paper strip using the template for your chosen flower. Using a sharp pair of scissors, snip across the width of the paper to make a fringe, leaving at least a 5mm (¼in) uncut from the bottom. Make sure you cut as straight a line as possible and try to fringe the paper into really thin strips, as this will create a more delicate-looking centre.

   Continue to snip until the whole width of the paper strip is fringed.

2. Apply a small line of glue to the bottom right side of the paper, then place your florist wire onto this and begin to tightly roll the paper around the wire, ensuring the tip of the wire is at least 1cm (½in) into the fringed stamen.

   At around the halfway point, apply a small amount of glue to the bottom of the paper strip and continue to roll – this will help secure the stamen and prevent it unravelling.

3. Continue to roll the paper until you are almost at the end, then apply a little bit of glue to secure it in place and roll the strip closed.

   Open up the top of the fringed centre by brushing a finger over it in different directions so it's not so tightly pressed together, which gives it a more realistic look.

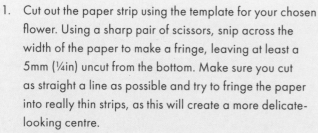

sculpting petals and leaves

The petals and leaves of a flower are what defines it, setting apart a delicate jasmine from a striking peony. A few very simple sculpting techniques can have the brilliant effect of creating lifelike paper flowers – it's all in a delicate fold or a gentle curl. Knowing the techniques for just four petals and four leaves will give you a good base for making any of the flowers in this book.

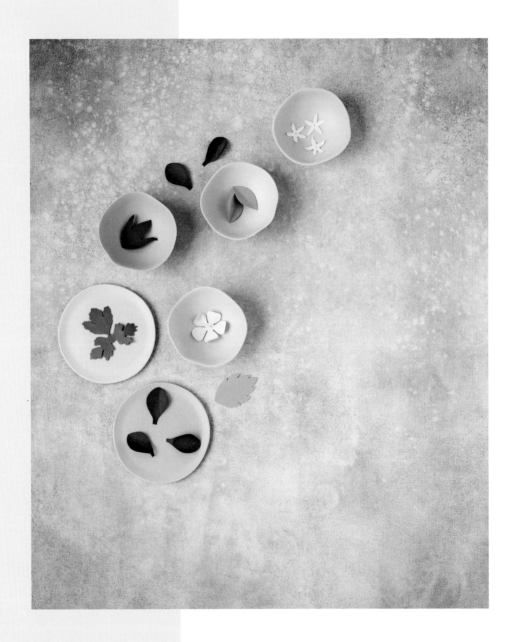

pleated petal

you will need:

Paper flower petals

1. Start by folding the petal lengthways down the centre, pressing down on the table if needed.

2. Now fold the left side of the petal back onto itself to create a pleat, then repeat until you reach the edge of the petal. The pleats pictured are roughly 1cm (½in) wide, but these can be made larger or smaller depending on the look you require and the size and width of your petals.

3. You can measure the width from the widest points of the first petal to see how many pleats and what size will fit your petals if you want to be precise, but this doesn't need to be exact and can just as easily and effectively be done by eye. Continue to pleat the other side of the petal, then repeat the process for all the other petals.

blossom
petal

you will need:

Paper blossom • Wooden skewer
or knitting needle

1. Take your paper blossom in one hand and place
    a skewer or knitting needle at the top of one of the
    blossom petals. Roll the paper petal inwards with
    the skewer inside until at least half of the petal is
    rolled up, then carefully remove the skewer. Repeat
    for all petals until the blossom is complete.

2. If you want a more open look, pull the petals
    outwards slightly.

3. A cocktail stick is really useful to roll the petals of very
    small blossom flowers, and easier than a larger skewer
    or needle. A bone folder can also be used in a similar
    way to give a more angled curl (see page 71).

small petal

you will need:

Wooden skewer or knitting
needle • Paper petals

1. Place a skewer or knitting needle
    on the side edge of the flower petals,
    pinch the edge of the paper over and
    onto the skewer and begin to tightly
    roll the petal around it.

2. Once the whole petal has been rolled
    up, carefully remove the skewer or
    knitting needle and open up the petal,
    taking care not to completely flatten
    the shape you have created. Repeat
    for all the petals.

large petal

you will need:

Wooden skewer or knitting needle • Paper petals

1. Place a skewer or knitting needle on the side edge of the petal, pinch the edge of the paper over and onto the skewer and begin to tightly roll the petal around it. Once the whole petal has been rolled up, carefully remove the skewer to leave the petal rolled up.

2. Begin to unroll one side of the petal, then place the skewer at the top of the petal at an angle. Carefully roll the petal over and around the skewer, then remove it gently to leave a curled edge. This can be done on the left or right side of the petal, and you can use a mixture of these for variety.

3. You can curl both sides of the petal if you like, too, then use a mixture of all three variations together, as in the paper rose centre (see page 96).

veined leaf

1. Fold the leaf down the centre lengthways.

2. Carefully fold the leaf in half and make a fold going from the top left side of the leaf into the folded middle section at a slant, as shown, then unfold to leave a crease mark.

   Repeat the last step twice, each time moving further down the leaf so you have three diagonal crease marks spaced along the leaf.

3. Open up the leaf, then repeat for all leaves.

single crease leaf

1. Dimension can be added to the most basic leaf shape, like that used for the cherry blossom (see page 82), by simply making a crease down the centre of the leaf, lengthways.

pointed leaf

1. Make a light crease lengthways from the top of the middle point to the bottom, and open up again, taking care not to fold and press down too hard.

2. Next, crease from the top left point to the bottom of the leaf to meet the crease from the first fold.

3. Repeat the last step for the right point and you are finished.

compound leaves

1. For compound shapes with multiple leaves, starting at the top, carefully crease down the middle of each leaf section, as shown. Take care not to completely fold the paper or the line will look too harsh.

2. Continue with all the leaves until each one is creased down the middle.

wiring a leaf

Once you have cut and shaped your chosen leaves, they will need to be attached to wire in preparation for being attached to the flower stem. There are three main ways to do this, and each achieves a different effect as to how the leaves look and behave. For example, the sandwich method results in a much sturdier leaf, which is necessary for the Hellebore (page 62), whereas a simple glued leaf is fine for use with the Jasmine (page 112).

you will need:

Hot glue gun and glue sticks • 30-gauge florist wire
Wire cutters • White tack • Pin or needle

single wire leaf

1. Lay the leaf down, wrong side up. Using a hot glue gun, apply a line of glue at the bottom of the leaf. Take the florist wire and immediately place it into the hot glue, keeping it pressed down in place until the glue has started to set and the wire is fixed securely.

sandwich wire leaf

1. Take two identical leaves that have been creased and shaped together, one on top of the other (see page 42).

2. Place the bottom leaf on the table, then using a hot glue gun apply a line of glue down the centre line of the leaf. Quickly place the florist wire into the hot glue and lay the top leaf onto it, sandwiching the two leaf parts together with the florist wire in between.

twisted wire leaf

1. Take a large ball of white tack and place it on the table in front of you. Put the paper leaf on top of the white tack and, using a pin or needle, pierce a hole into the bottom of the leaf, ensuring it's as central as possible and not too close to the edge as it may tear at a later stage.

2. Take a piece of 30 gauge florist wire and push it through the hole towards the top of the leaf.

3. Pull the top of the wire downwards, folding it in half to meet the bottom half of the wire.

   Carefully twist the two wires together, making sure the start of the twist is close to the bottom of the leaf's edge and that you don't tear the paper as you go.

   Trim off any excess wire with cutters but leave enough so that you can attach the leaf to a wire stem.

ranunculus

The ranunculus is a very simple flower to craft. It's made from one continuous spiral of paper and there isn't much intricate, time-consuming cutting to be done, so it's a great place to start learning to make paper flowers. These can be made in a variety of colours, but making a few flowers out of different shades of one colour makes a lovely selection, such as these yellow and orange ones. You could also try shades of pink. The ranunculus stems look wonderful displayed in simple vases, either individually or as a group.

you will need:

Ranunculus templates (page 128) • Pencil • Paper – green and your preferred petal colours • Small sharp scissors • Wooden skewer Hot glue gun and glue sticks • White tack • Large needle Cotton bud • Florist wire (24-gauge) Green florist tape • Bone folder

instructions:

1. Photocopy the ranunculus flower template onto your chosen paper or photocopy it onto some heavyweight paper and cut it out, then draw around it on your chosen paper. Do the same with the leaf using green paper and attach a wire stem with the single wire technique (page 46).

   Take the end of the spiral-shaped flower template and tightly curl the paper spiral around a skewer until you reach the centre (see page 40). Hold in place for a minute or so before carefully removing the skewer – this will help the paper keep the spiral shape.

   Using the hot glue gun, apply some glue to the middle of the spiral, leaving the very centre glue-free. Taking care not to burn your fingers, place the tightly rolled spiral onto the glue and hold it in place whilst it sets. Set aside.

   Following the instructions on page 30, make a bud stamen, but only cover the cotton bud in florist tape, not the whole wire.

2. Take the ranunculus flower head and place it face down in the palm of your hand. Using a pin or needle, carefully pierce a hole in the very centre, just big enough to fit the wrire stem through.

3. Take the bud stamen and apply hot glue to the area between the plastic cotton bud base and the wire. While the glue is still hot, insert the wire stem through the hole in the centre of the flower head and push through until the stamen is as far down into the centre of the spiral as possible. Hold in place until the glue is set.

    Take some florist tape and begin wrapping the stem of the flower from the top down (see page 25). Place a leaf at around 6cm (2¼in) from the flower and wrap its stem tightly to the main flower stem using the tape. Continue wrapping the flower stem until you reach the bottom, then cut or twist off the tape.

flower bouquet

This mixed flower bouquet would look beautiful in any home or make a great gift – it can even be wrapped in brown paper with a gift tag attached like real flowers. This arrangement would also look good in one colour; why not try making it in shades of yellow for a spring feel?

you will need:

Selection of paper flowers of different sizes and leaves or foliage
Length of twine • Scissors • Wire cutters • Ribbon (optional)

1. To make a paper flower bouquet, select the flowers you wish to use, including any extra leaves or foliage you would like to incorporate. (In the large bouquet here, single peony leaves on long wires have been used to add in some greenery.)

2. Have your twine cut and to hand before you begin. Start off by selecting a few of the larger flowers and holding them in one hand, then add in smaller flowers to fill the space between the larger blooms. Keep going in this way until you have a bouquet you are happy with. Now take any extra green foliage you would like to incorporate and add this into the mix.

3. Keep hold of the flowers in one hand and with the other take a length of twine and tightly wrap the flower stems, going around several times, until they feel securely in place. Tie the twine into a knot and then a bow. If the flower stems move around, cut the twine and re-tie.

4. Take a pair of wire cutters and trim the wire stems so that they are all the same length. Tie a ribbon bow around the stems, if you wish, as a finishing touch.

poppy

This bloom is inspired by the Icelandic poppy. The simple technique of pleating petals adds great texture and dimension to a paper flower, and this method would also work well with different paper types, such as tissue paper or vellum.

Poppies make lovely feature when displayed with a mixture of other flowers and foliage, as in the table garland (page 110).

you will need:

Poppy templates (page 129) • Peach, yellow, mint and green paper
Pencil • Small sharp scissors • Green florist tape • Crepe or
tissue paper • Hot glue gun and glue sticks
20-gauge florist wire

instructions:

1. Photocopy 12 petal and 2 leaf templates of your chosen shape onto your chosen paper, or photocopy all the templates onto some heavyweight paper and cut them out, then draw around them on your chosen paper. Cut out the stamen and fringe templates.

   Make the poppy ball stamen using the directions on page 31, only wrapping the first inch of the top of the stem for now. Take 2 of the thin strips of paper for the stamen star, and, using a very small bead of glue, attach each end of the strip to the bottom of the stamen, creating a cross shape over the top of it. Take the 2 remaining strips and repeat in the spaces between to create a star shape in the centre. Set aside.

2. Cut the yellow stamen strip using the fringing technique on page 32. Apply some glue to one end of the fringed paper and attach to the outside of the bud. Wrap around the ball and secure at the other end with a dab of glue.

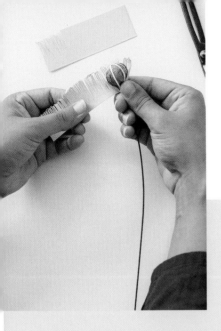

3. Pleat the flower petals following the
    directions on page 38, making sure the
    folds are as evenly spaced as possible
    – starting from the middle and working
    outwards may help.

    Using your fingers, gently flatten the
    bottom of each petal so it has more contact
    when glued to the stamen. Apply some hot
    glue to the bottom of a petal and stick it to
    the ball centre, then attach 5 more petals
    all the way around the centre, making sure
    they're evenly spaced. Then attach the last 6
    petals underneath in another layer, placing
    the first petal under and between 2 petals
    above, so the overall look is staggered.

4. Wire the leaves using the single wire leaf
    technique on page 46. Wrap the stem of the
    flower from the top downwards with green
    florist tape, attaching the leaves to the stem
    as you go (see pages 25–26).

gift topper

This poppy gift topper is made from second-hand sheet music pages and the outer cover of the book they came from. I carefully placed the poppy templates over the sections of text, print and music notes I wanted to include. You can use any found paper you like to make this gift topper, though; old maps, book pages or even letters can make fantastic decorative and attractive toppers.

Any of the flowers in this book can be made from found papers in a similar way and used to add a little something extra to your gift.

you will need:

Poppy templates (page 129) • Sheet music or other found papers
Pencil • Small sharp scissors • Crepe or tissue paper • Hot glue gun and glue sticks • Florist wire • Wire cutters • Pliers • Brown paper
Twine • Sticky fixer (optional)

1. Take the poppy templates and place onto the part of the paper you would like to feature on the flower. Make up a paper poppy using the tutorial on page 58, wrapping the stem in more found paper and attaching the leaves.

2. Take a pair of pliers and bend the poppy head so that when the stem is lying flat on top of the gift the flower head faces upwards, as shown.

3. Wrap your gift in brown paper and tie with twine, leaving a little excess at the top of the gift.

4. Place the poppy on top of your gift and trim the wire stem so it fits without hanging over the edge too much.

5. To secure the poppy to the gift wrap, tie the excess twine around the poppy stem and tie into place, or if you prefer, use a sticky fixer tab or similar to stick the poppy head down onto the gift.

hellebore

This hellebore-inspired flower is eye-catching as a single stem but it also looks great displayed en masse, as on the tiered cake decoration on page 66.

It looks lovely in any colour but it is particularly striking in this dark purple shade.

you will need:

Hellebore templates (page 130) • Dark purple and dark green paper
Pencil • Small sharp scissors • Florist wire (20- and 22-gauge)
Wooden skewer • Hot glue gun and glue sticks • Green florist tape

instructions:

1. Photocopy 6 petal and 4 large leaf and 4 small leaf templates onto your chosen paper, or photocopy all the templates onto some heavyweight paper and cut them out, then draw around them on your chosen paper. Cut out the stamen templates.

   Crease the leaves and wire them using the sandwich technique (see page 46) to make 2 large and 2 small wired leaves. Using a wooden skewer, curl the hellebore petals lengthways (see page 40). Hold the flower petals between your finger and thumb, then using the other hand bend the bottom of the petal downwards to create a flat edge to glue.

2. Take the scissors and cut the flower stamen using the fringing technique on page 32. Using a piece of 20-gauge wire, first roll

the smaller, thinner-fringed stamen around the wire then wrap in the second, thicker-fringed stamen on top.

3. Apply a small amount of glue to the flat edge of a petal and stick it onto the flower centre. Continue with the remaining petals, spacing them evenly around the stamen.

4. Wrap the stem of the flower from the top downwards with green florist tape, attaching the leaves as you go using the florist tape (see pages 25–26).

cake decoration

This hellebore flower topper is a pretty and inexpensive way to make any cake look really special. If you prefer, use a mixture of different flowers, such as ranunculus and asters, which would also look great.

you will need:

Hellebore templates (page 130) • Selection of papers
Cocktail sticks • Hot glue gun and glue sticks

1. Following the hellebore flower tutorial on page 64, make up 13 flowers using a cocktail stick instead of the florist wire as a stem, and without wrapping them in florist tape. Stick the leaves directly onto the side of the flower heads using a hot glue gun.

2. Begin to place the flowers on your cake by pushing the cocktail stick in as far as it will go. Use the flowers in the picture for inspiration as to how to arrange them, or if you are feeling a little more adventurous, why not try a different design?

chrysanthemum

The chrysanthemum flower is made up of lots of layers, making it a really full-looking bloom. Despite this, the construction is very straightforward, so it's a quick larger flower to make up as part of a bouquet or large display.

Why not try making a collection of these in a bright yellow for a vibrant look?

you will need:

Chrysanthemum templates (pages 130–31) • Pale yellow and green paper Pencil • Small sharp scissors • Florist wire (18- and 24-gauge) Bone folder • White tack • Pin or needle • Hot glue gun and glue sticks • Pliers • Green florist tape

instructions:

1. Photocopy 3 large outer petals, 3 medium inner petals, 8 small inner petals, 1 central petal strip, 1 small circle and 2 leaf templates onto your chosen paper, or photocopy all the templates onto some heavyweight paper and cut them out, then draw around them on your chosen paper.

   Wire the leaves using the twisted wire technique on page 47. Set aside.

   Using a bone folder, curl all the petals by carefully grasping each one between your thumb and the edge of the bone folder and firmly pulling towards you from the middle, similar to curling a plastic ribbon using the back of scissor blades.

2. Take a ball of white tack and a pin or needle. Place each petal onto the white tack and use the pin to pierce a hole in the centre, large enough for the wire stem to fit through.

3. Take the inner petal strip and curl it using a bone folder, then carefully wrap it into a spiral and secure into place with a small amount of glue at one end.

4. Slowly thread all the large petals onto the 18-gauge wire stem, making sure the petals are curled upwards, applying a small amount of glue to each around the hole in the centre as you go and pressing each petal onto the one above. Be careful not to glue the petals to the stem at this point. Continue with the medium and small petals. Ensure the petals are staggered and not in line with the one above.

5. Using a pair of pliers, carefully bend the wire stem flat at the top of the flower so it sits flush with the inside of the flower, and hold in place. Apply glue to the wire at the top and carefully place the small yellow circle over the top, holding it in place until the glue is set.

6. Dab some glue onto the small yellow circle in the centre of the flower and stick on the curled inner petal strip.

7. Wrap florist tape around the wire stem and attach the leaves as you go (see page 26).

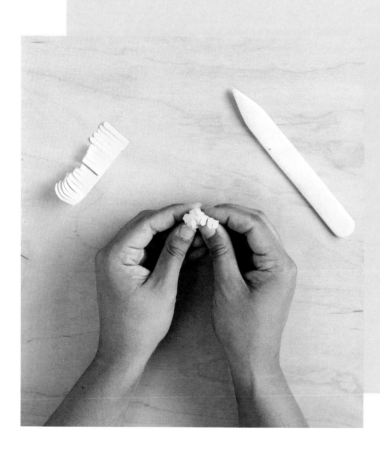

floral stairway

This floral installation down a staircase is a great way to show off lots of different types flowers all together in one stunning display. It would make a beautiful feature at a wedding or special event and a great background for photos to be taken in front of.

Use thick 3.5mm (0.14in) thick garden wire or alternatively a strong florist wire to create a base for the larger flowers at the bottom, then build this up with more and more flowers. If they're made on long stems then the wire can wrap around the stairs and hold them in place, or just tape and glue the flowers together.

For a more festive look why not try neutral colours mixed with gold and silver for a winter-themed decoration?

aster

The pretty lavender-blue flowers of the aster, or Michaelmas daisy, remind me of my late grandma, whose favourite colour was lilac. These are really quick to make, as the flower itself is just two strips of fringed paper tightly wrapped around a stem. You can use these in a variety of ways – either on their own as a bunch in a small bottle or vase, or incorporated into a larger arrangement of other flowers, as in the wreath (page 118).

As an alternative colourway, these daisies would also look great with a yellow centre surrounded by white petals.

you will need:

Aster templates (page 132) • Lilac, yellow and green paper
Pencil • Small sharp scissors • Hot glue gun
and glue sticks • Florist wire (22-gauge)
Green florist tape

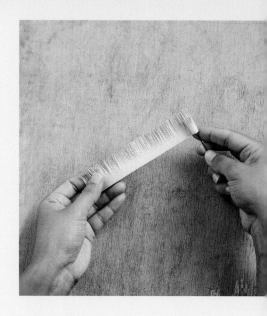

instructions:

1. Photocopy 12 petal strip, 40 leaf and 12 stamen templates onto
    your chosen paper, or photocopy all the templates onto some
    heavyweight paper and cut them out, then draw around them on
    your chosen paper.

    Make the stamen using the fringing method on page 32 with
    the 22-gauge wire.

2. Using the same fringing technique, fringe the lilac petal strip,
    leaving at least 5mm (¼in) at the bottom – make sure you
    don't cut too far down the paper as this will make the petals
    fragile and more difficult to wrap around the centre. Apply a
    small amount of glue onto one end of the petals and place the
    prepared stamen onto the glue. Make sure the unfringed bottom
    of the stamen and petals are level with each other. Roll the
    fringed lilac petals around the stamen, applying glue to secure
    them at the end.

3. Gently bend the lilac petals outwards to create the shape of
    the flower.

4. Turn the flower upside down and apply some hot glue around the wire and paper at the bottom of the flower head, then leave to dry. This will reinforce the structure and keep everything in place.

5. Once the glue is dry, take some green florist tape and wrap the base of the flower head, continuing down the wire stem and taking care to cover any paper that might be showing (see page 26).

    Set aside some single stems, then group the rest into threes and wrap them together using florist tape (see page 26). Leave the flower stems to dry – preferably overnight, as the florist tape can be sticky, which makes it more difficult to attach the aster leaves directly onto them.

6. Crease the leaves lengthways down the centre (see page 43), then once the tape has dried out apply a small bead of hot glue at the bottom of each leaf (the rounded end) and stick them directly onto the top half of the flower stem, one leaf opposite another. Display the stems grouped all together.

hanging leaves

This hanging leaf display is easy to create from a few basic materials, most of which can be found around the house. Make it on a larger scale by using a bigger, longer twig or tree branch and more rows of leaves; or use longer leaf garlands and create a backdrop or feature for an event or party.

Changing the colourway will give the whole display a completely different look. Try using oranges, browns and yellows for an autumnal look, or add in some flower shapes between the leaves for a pop of colour.

you will need:

Variety of paper leaves • White tack • Pin or needle • 30-gauge wire or a reel of very thin wire • Long twig or small branch • Twine • Scissors

1. To make these hanging leaves you need a selection of leaf shapes in various colours. You can use the leaf templates from this book or use a real leaf to draw around onto some card, cut it out and make your own template.

2. Place each leaf onto a lump of white tack or similar and pierce a hole into the bottom of the leaf or stem using a pin. The hole needs to be big enough for the thin wire. Now thread your wire through the hole in your first leaf, leaving at least a few centimetres of excess wire at the end.

3. Hold the leaf between your thumb and forefinger whilst keeping the threaded wire in place, then thread the wire through the hole a second time and carefully pull it through, making sure you don't tear the delicate paper edge of the leaf. Repeat with the second leaf – for the larger leaves, place the second leaf further up the wire so the bottom tip of the leaf is just meeting the top of the leaf below. For small leaves, place the second leaf to the side of the first. Repeat until all the leaves are on the wire.

4. Take the branch and place the leaf chains onto it in a formation of your choice. Wrap the wire around the branch several times to secure the leaves in place, then twist the end of the wire around the hanging wire and cut off any excess.

5. Cut a length of twine and tie each end to either side of the branch so you can hang it up to display.

cherry blossom

Cherry blossom is simple yet beautiful. It can be used to create a stunning display for the home by suspending multiple branches from a height, or the delicate blossom can also be arranged in a simple vase or glass bottles to make a lovely feature for a mantlepiece or side table.

These blossoms look great in white, pale yellow or really any colour – make them to suit the occasion or your colour scheme.

you will need:

Cherry blossom templates (page 132) • Light pink, green and pale yellow paper • Pencil • Small sharp scissors • Wooden skewer White tack • Pin or needle • Florist wire (24-gauge) • Hot glue gun and glue sticks • Green and brown florist tape • Small tree branch

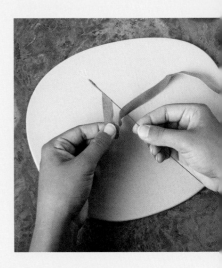

instructions:

1. Photocopy the cherry blossom flower, leaf and stamen templates onto your chosen paper so that you have 40 of each, or photocopy all the templates onto some heavyweight paper and cut them out, then draw around them on your chosen paper. Carefully crease each leaf down the centre lengthways (see page 43), taking care not to press down too hard to create a harsh-looking fold – a creased line looks more natural.

2. Snip 6 thin strips into each stamen. Tightly roll it up so the fringes are gathered together. Repeat to create 40 small flower stamens.

   Cut 40 5-cm (2-in) lengths of 24-gauge wire. Using a hot glue gun, apply a small amount of glue to the end of each wire and wrap the bottom of each stamen around the wire. Using florist tape, wrap the bottom third of the stamen and continue wrapping onto the wire (see page 25). Repeat with all 40 stamen.

3. Using a skewer, curl each petal inwards, carefully uncurling them slightly as the skewer is removed.

   One by one, place each blossom flower onto a ball of white tack and pierce a small hole that's just big enough for the stamen to be pushed through.

4. Take the stamen and push the wire through the hole in the centre of the cherry blossom, carefully pushing the wrapped part of the stamen through as well. Apply some hot glue to the underside of the flower head to secure the stamen and wire stem in place and to attach it to the flower.

5. Take 2–3 blossoms at a time and place them onto a real tree branch, using brown florist tape to attach the flower stems to it (see page 26). Make sure you leave some space between the flower groups for the leaves to be attached.

6. Bend the bottom tip of each leaf and apply some hot glue, then attach the leaf to the branch quickly before the glue sets, holding it in place for a few seconds.

   If you want a fuller look, or if there are any sparse areas on the branch, add more cherry blossoms or leaves.

hanging
cherry blossom

These cherry blossom branches are a favourite of mine. They are so versatile when it comes to displaying them, suspended from above they make a stunning feature over a mantle. They would work equally as well over a dining table as a new take on a floral centrepiece.

Simply forage your local woodland or parks for some suitably shaped and sized fallen branches, then use a hot glue gun to attach the flowers and foliage. Hang with twine or wire, depending on the effect you want to create.

The blossom colour and even the types of flower can be changed. Any paper flower can be attached to real branches, so why not experiment and try a mixture of small blooms and see what you can come up with?

mini posy set
of three

These mini flower posies are pretty and make lovely gifts. They can be used as bridesmaid's flowers and can double up as a gift for after the wedding.

Any colourway can be used – why not try making these in white or ivory and adding a personalised tag and a spritz of perfume to make them extra special?

you will need:

16 small paper flowers (I've used hellebore, small rose buds and cherry blossoms, see pages 62, 96 and 82) • Length of twine • Scissors • Wire cutters
Ribbon (optional) • Gift tag (optional)

1. Group together a mixture of hellebore, small rose buds and cherry blossoms on stems in different colours, or use a mixture of your own favourite flowers. Arrange the flowers so their heads are in a round posy shape, pushing down any that sit higher than the others so they are more even, and move any flowers that you feel need repositioning now.

2. Once you have the flowers in an arrangement that you are happy with, keep a hold of them with one hand, take a length of twine and begin to wrap the stems tightly, about halfway up. Once they feel secure, tie the twine into a bow. If the flower stems move around, cut the twine and re-tie them.

3. Take a pair of wire cutters and trim the stems so they are all one length. Take a minute to rearrange any flowers that need adjusting by separating the flower heads slightly and re-forming the circular shape if they have moved whilst being tied.

4. Repeat the process for the next two posies.

5. If you like, you can use a ribbon instead of twine to tie the posy, but be aware that it can slip, allowing the flowers to move around. It's best to use twine to wrap then tie the ribbon on top.

bluebell

The bluebell looks complex but is in fact surprisingly simple to make; the bell shape takes a little time and patience to put together, but once you've made the first flower all will become clear.

These are oversized bluebells as the real flowers are quite tiny, however, if you are feeling like a challenge after making these a few times, the templates can be copied and reduced by 50 per cent to create something similar in size to the real thing.

you will need:

Bluebell templates (page 132) • Lilac and dark green paper
Pencil • Small sharp scissors • Bone folder • Wooden skewer
Hot glue gun and glue sticks • Florist wire (22- and 24-gauge)
Green florist tape

91   bluebell

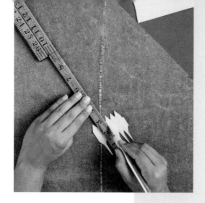

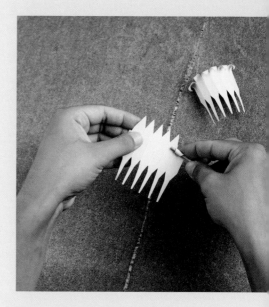

instructions:

1. Photocopy 12 bluebell flowers and 10 leaf templates onto your chosen paper, or photocopy all the templates onto some heavyweight paper and cut them out, then draw around them on your chosen paper.

   Take the flower shape and score along the lines shown, including the small tab at the side. Take care not to press down too hard and cut through the paper. Fold each score line so that the scored side of the paper is facing outwards.

2. Using a skewer, curl the short pointed edges of the flower outwards (see page 39). These will be the petals.

3. Apply a small amount of glue to the tab at the side and attach to the opposite side so the flower forms a tube.

4. Place a 22-gauge wire inside the bell shape, making sure the wire doesn't stick out the other end past the curledpetals. Gather the long thin strips on the flower together, pinch tightly around the wire stem and hold it with one hand. With the other hand, take some green florist tape and wrap it tightly around the long thin strips and wire stem (see page 25), ensuring the

flower head is attached securely to the stem. Undo and repeat if necessary, as this can be tricky. Repeat for all the flowers.

5. Bend each flower head over to one side. Then, for one stem, group the flowers in two groups of 3 and 2 and join these together using florist tape (see page 26). Place the bunch of 2 behind but above the bunch of 3 and secure them using florist tape. Now place 1 single flower behind but above the bunch of 2 and attach to create a tiered effect. Repeat for the second bluebell stem.

6. Using a bone folder, curl the leaves at the top pointed edge. Place and attach the leaves onto the stem using florist tape (see page 26, although these leaves are on a wire, the method is the same).

mini bluebell plant

This mini plant is a great way of using old books to create a small display. This bluebell looks great on its own but would also work well in a group. Why not try making a little trio of different flowers, standing them each in a different book? You can display this little plant on a shelf or mantle in your home, or on top of a stack of books as a centrepiece for a wedding or dinner table.

you will need:

Bluebell templates (see page 90) • Small second-hand book
Thick cream or ivory card • Scissors • Glue stick • Pliers
Hot glue gun and glue sticks • Wire cutters

1. First, reduce the bluebell template by 50% and use them to make one small paper bluebell stem using the tutorial on page 90.

2. Use some of the pages from the book of your choice for the flowers, if you like, or, if you prefer, colour copy some of the pages to use instead, copying onto both sides of your plain paper.

3. Cut the thick card to the same size as your book pages, then take a page from the book or a photocopy of it and stick it to the card using a glue stick.

4. Take the stem of your bluebell bunch and bend the bottom until it's in an L shape using a pair of pliers. Apply a generous amount of hot glue to the bottom part of the 'L' and stick the bluebell stem onto the card base you have just created, so the flower stands up off the page. Apply more hot glue to stabilise the stem if needed.

5. Take another page from the book or a copied page and cut some short, thin strips of paper. Stick these strips over and around the wire base of the flower to hide it, using the hot glue gun. Place the strips in a non-uniform way, overlapping each other as you would with papier-mâché. This not only hides the wire but also provides a more stable base for the bluebell to stand on.

6. Open the book in the place you would like to display the bluebell and place or glue the book-page-covered card into the book.

7. Display the book either on its own or on a pile of other books for a bit more height.

rose

This is my favourite flower to craft. Every time I make one
I remember all the beautiful roses growing in my mum's garden
when I was a child, and collecting the soft velvety petals to keep.

A rose works well as a single flower or a few clustered together
as a bouquet. This tutorial makes a single stem with a large rose
and a smaller opening rose bud. It also looks great in any colour
and printed paper; for the perfect gift and keepsake, use found
papers such as old letters, book pages or even old maps.

you will need:

Rose templates (page 136) • Off-white or ivory and green paper
Pencil • Small sharp scissors • Florist wire (18- and 24-gauge)
Green florist tape • Wooden skewer • Hot glue gun
and glue sticks

instructions:

1. For the main large rose, photocopy two 5-petal templates,
    one 4-petal template, one 3-petal template and eight
    of the single-petal templates onto your chosen paper, or
    photocopy all the templates onto some heavyweight paper
    and cut them out, then draw around them on your chosen
    paper. Repeat for the small rose templates, but note that
    this does not have the 5-petal shape.

    Next, cut out 6 small leaves and 6 large leaves. Attach
    wires to each leaf using the sandwich technique (see page
    46) so you have 3 small and 3 large finished leaves.
    Using florist tape (see page 26) attach the 3 small leaves
    together and fan out, then repeat with the large leaves.
    Set these aside.

    Take a wooden skewer and carefully curl all the outer
    rose petals on the top left and right side around the skewer
    (see page 39), but don't curl the single petals.

2. Next curl the single petals around the skewer, one by one. Begin at the side of the petal, making sure it is held lengthways, and roll the entire petal around the skewer (see page 40).

3. Once all 8 petals are curled, place 2 to one side to remain fully curled. Take 2 petals and curl the top left and right (in the same way as with the outer petals). Curl another 2 on the left side only and a further 2 on the right side only (see page 41). This will give a more natural look to the petals and add more interest to the centre of the flower.

4. Take the 2 fully curled petals (that are still tightly rolled up), apply a small amount of glue to the bottom part of one and tightly wrap around an 18-gauge wire. Repeat with the second petal, placing it over the top of the first petal and making sure the bottom of each petal is in line with the others.

5. Now take the remaining 6 single petals and arrange them around the centre of the flower by applying glue to the bottom of each and placing them around the centre of the rose. You can add these in any order but make sure they are always level with each other and fit tightly, with the bottom part near the wire.

6. Apply a small amount of glue to the tab on each of the larger petal shapes and stick to the opposite side, making sure the tab is on the back of the flower shape. Take a sharp pair of scissors and cut a hole in the bottom of each to allow a space through which you can put the stem and the bottom of the flower centre.

7. Apply hot glue all the way around the bottom of the flower centre near the wire stem and quickly thread on the 3-petal shape, then hold them in place until the glue sets. If there is a lot of space between the flower centre and the 3 petals, squeeze the bottom of the petals to close this gap before the glue dries. Repeat for the remaining petals.

8. To make the smaller opening bud, just repeat all the above steps (note, this smaller rose doesn't have the two 5 petals).

9. Join the 2 flower stems together using green florist tape (see page 26), then attach the two sets of leaves to the main stem.

   Bend each flower head over to one side to give a more natural look, and arrange and shape the leaves so that you are happy with how they are displayed.

hair clip

This rose hair clip would be perfect for a wedding. Why not make matching rose posies to go with it using the posy tutorial from page 88? Great for bridesmaids or a flower girl.

you will need:

Small rose templates (see page 96) • Wire cutters
Florist tape • Pliers • Green paper • Scissors • Metal hair clip
Hot glue gun and glue sticks

1. Make up 2 small roses and 3 small leaves from the tutorial on page 96.

2. Hold the 2 roses together, and using florist tape join the 2 stems, wrapping them from just below the flower heads to around 5cm (2in) down the stems (see page 26). Place the 3 leaves around the roses, as seen in the picture, and tape the leaf wires to the rose stem.

3. Using pliers, tightly curl the wire stem into a spiral from the bottom up to the top and push the curled wire up so it sits near the flower heads tucked out of the way.

4. Take the green paper and cut it just long and wide enough to cover the top of the metal hair clip. Glue this directly onto the top of the metal hair clip using a hot glue gun. This will hide the metal and become the base for you to stick the roses and leaves onto.

5. Apply some hot glue onto the 2 leaves at the sides of the roses and stick onto the paper base you have just made. Hold in place until the glue is set.

peony

The peony is slightly different to the other flowers in this book, as the petals are crumpled rather than curled to give the characteristic, delicate, tissue-like effect of their petals.

This flower makes a real statement as a single stem and also looks really effective as part of a bigger floral display, such as the table garland decoration on page 110. It also looks great in a darker shade of pink or fuchsia.

you will need

Peony templates (pages 134–36) • Dusky pink, yellow and green paper • Pencil • Small sharp scissors • Hot glue gun and glue sticks Florist wire (24-gauge) • Crepe or tissue paper • Bone folder Green florist tape

1. Photocopy 8 leaves, three large 5-petal shapes, two large 4-petal shape, 6 single petals and 12 long thin inner petals onto your chosen paper, or photocopy all the templates onto some heavyweight paper and cut them out, then draw around them on your chosen paper.

    Cut out 8 peony leaf shapes, fold using the compound leaf technique on page 42 and wire using the sandwich technique on page 46 to make 4 leaves. Copy the stamen strip template onto yellow paper. Take a sharp pair of scissors and create the flower stamen using the fringing technique on page 32.

2. Carefully scrunch all of the petals – do this one by one, even on the larger petal shapes, taking care not to tear the paper as you go. Apply a small amount of glue to the tab on the larger petal shapes and stick to the opposite side, making sure the tab is on the back of the flower shape. Using scissors, cut a hole in the bottom of each of the flower shapes to allow space for the stem and flower stamen to be pushed into.

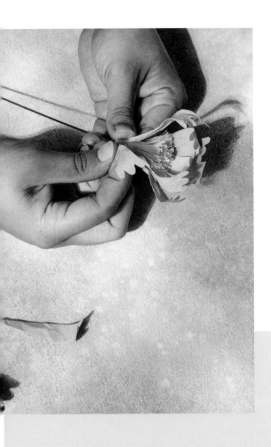

3. Take the small, long, thin inner petals and apply a small amount of glue to the bottom, stick them onto the flower stamen, overlapping them slightly and making sure they are evenly spaced.

4. Next, glue the single petals onto the flower centre in the same way, ensuring all the petals are level.

5. Apply some glue to the bottom of the flower centre you have created and push the wire through the 3-petal shape until the flower centre is inside the petal shape, then hold in place until the glue is dry. Repeat with the remaining petal shapes.

6. To make the peony bud, cut out 3 of the round peony bud petals and 3 of the bud calyx in green paper. Carefully scrunch the paper, then gently unfold it.

   Roll up a ball of crepe or tissue paper to the size of a ping-pong ball. Apply a generous amount of glue to the ball and stick an 18-gauge wire onto it, pushing the wire into the crepe paper and holding it in place until the glue is set. Make sure the wire is securely in place; you can apply more glue if it needs reinforcing.

7. Take a single bud petal and pinch it on one side, apply a small amount of glue inside, then fold over the pinched area and glue down to create a small cupped shape. Repeat with the 2 other petals.

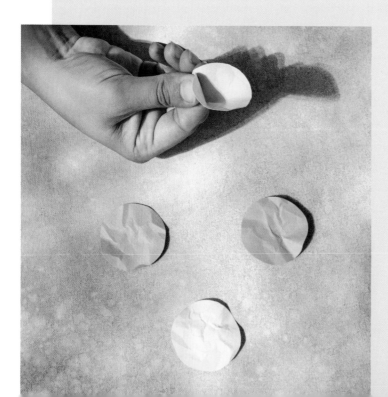

8. Glue the cupped petals onto the crepe paper ball, ensuring that you cover the top and side of the ball so the crepe paper isn't visible. Take the 3 green calyx and curl them upwards using the side of a bone folder (see page 71). Apply glue to the calyx evenly and secure onto the base and sides of the bud.

9. Now attach the stem of the main flower to the stem of the bud using florist tape (see page 26). Shape the stems by bending over to one side slightly. Attach the leaves using florist tape – see the techniques on page 26 – and arrange to your liking.

table garland

This garland can be used in a variety of ways and, as it is flexible, it is easy to manipulate into a shape to suit any space. It makes a beautiful focal point for a dinner table, but it could also be arranged over a mantle or even on a stairway, tied onto a banister rail.

You can change the flowers and foliage to suit your theme or your chosen colourway. Why not try making it out of metallic papers for a festive shimmer?

you will need:

Thick, flexible, PVC-coated garden wire (3.5mm/0.14in wide) • Wire cutters
Masking tape • Paper flowers • Green florist tape • Selection of green paper
leaves and foliage with long wires glued to the back • Scissors • Pliers

1. Measure out a 2.5m (8ft) length of thick, PVC-coated garden wire or similar, or measure the surface you are going to decorate and adjust the length accordingly, ensuring you add 50cm (20in) extra for securing the wire with an anchor point.

2. Take a small piece of masking tape and wrap it around the wire 50cm (20in) from the end of the side you will be starting on, then take another small piece of tape and wrap it 1m (3ft) further down the wire so you have a marker for the start point and the middle point of the 2m (6½ft) garland (if your garland is a different size, place the second marker at its halfway point).

3. Take the excess wire at one end and wrap it around a table leg to secure it into place – this will keep the wire anchored and make it easier to add your flowers and foliage.

4. Split all of your flowers and foliage into two groups so you know how much you have to work with for each half of the garland (if you would like the garland to appear symmetrical, make sure you have equal amounts of each flower for both sets).

5. Place one group of flowers and foliage on the floor in a line alongside your garden wire as you would like them to appear on the garland – move them around until you have a design you are happy with.

6. With your florist tape and wire cutters to hand, take two or three leaves or pieces of foliage at a time and hold them against the wire base. Using florist tape wrap them tightly to secure into place, positioning the leaves on either side of the wire base. Once attached, spread the leaves apart but make sure they overlap slightly to give a full look. If your leaf wires are too long, trim them shorter as you go. (See page 26 for how to attach leaves to a stem.)

7. Take your flowers and, using a pair of pliers, bend the flower head so it faces upwards when the stem is against the wire base. Cut any excess wire off the stem. Place the flower on top of the leaf base, and attach the flowers as you did the leaf wires, making sure it is secure and doesn't move around. Taping the flower stem onto the base can be a little fiddly as you will need to work between the leaf wire, so be patient and take your time, with a little practice you will find a method that works. Carry on in this way until you reach the end of your wire base.

8. Adjust the flowers and leaves so they sit nicely on the garland, lifting up some of the leaves so they aren't lying flat. If you see any areas that look sparse you can go back and add in a little more foliage.

9. Cut off the excess wire at the start of the garland, and you are finished!

jasmine

These tiny flowers are straightforward but do require patience to make the required quantity. So, put the kettle on and take your time, as the finished sprig is well worth the effort.

This can be added to at any time, so you can grow it into a bigger, more extravagant display. You can also change the colour of the blossoms to give a completely different look, like the orange flowers used in the wreath on page 118.

you will need

Jasmine templates (page 133) • White and green paper • Pencil
Small sharp scissors • Florist wire (22- and 30-gauge) • Hot glue gun
and glue sticks • Wooden skewer • White tack • Pin or needle
Green florist tape • Small plant pot • Decorative stones or gravel

instructions:

1. Photocopy 50 jasmine flowers and 60 leaf templates onto your chosen paper, or photocopy all the templates onto some heavyweight paper and cut them out, then draw around them on your chosen paper. Cut 110 10-cm (4-in) lengths from the 30-gauge wire.

   Fold each of the leaves down the centre lengthways and glue a strip of 30-gauge wire onto the back of each leaf using a hot glue gun (see page 46). Set aside.

   Using a wooden skewer, carefully curl the petals on each small jasmine flower (see page 39).

2. Roll a piece of white tack into a ball and place it on the table in front of you. One by one, place each jasmine flower on the white tack, with the petals curled back towards the white tack, and push down into the centre of the flower with the flat, circular end of the skewer so the centre of the flower curves downwards and the petals are pushed up.

With the flower still on the white tack, take a pin and pierce a hole in the very centre of the flower that's big enough to fit the 30-gauge wire stem through. Repeat for all 50 flowers.

3. When all the flowers are prepared, take one and push a piece of the 30-gauge wire through the hole in the centre.

4. Wrap the top of the wire stem around a thicker piece of 18-gauge wire twice so that you have two very small loops in the top of the wire stem.

5. Squeeze the loops together if there is any space between them.

6. Using a hot glue gun, apply a very small bead of glue to the bottom of the two wire loops then immediately pull the wire from the bottom of the stem down so that the loops stick to the centre of the flower and stay in place, creating the centre of the flower. Repeat for all flowers.

7. Bunch together 5 or 6 jasmine flowers and leaves, repeating with all the flowers so you have 9 bunches in total. Secure each bunch using florist tape (see page 26).

8. Take an 18-gauge wire and attach a bunch of the jasmine to the top of the wire using florist tape. Attach the next bunch lower down the wire, about 4cm (1½in) apart, and angle the jasmine slightly to the left. Repeat with the next bunch, angling the jasmine slightly to the right, and continue until they are all attached.

9. Once all the jasmine leaves and flowers have been attached, carefully shape the main plant stem over to one side so it looks more natural.

10. Depending on how you space the jasmine clusters and the length of your florist wire, you may need to add on more wire using florist tape if it isn't long enough. Ensure you overlap the wire by 5cm (2 in) before wrapping in florist tape so the main stem of the plant is secure. Allow enough wire at the bottom of the plant to reach the bottom of your plant pot or container.

11. Fill a small, decorative plant pot or jar with the stones of your choice and carefully push the jasmine plant stem into the stones until it reaches the bottom of the pot.

wreath

This looks great hung up or used flat as a table centrepiece. A collection of three wreaths would look wonderful hung along a hallway or over a mantle.

you will need:

Poppy and ranunculus leaf templates (page 128) • Paper for flowers and leaves • Hot glue gun and glue sticks • Florist wire • Cherry blossom, Aster and Jasmine flower templates (pages 132 and 133) • Large dinner plate or similar circular object • Thick, flexible, PVC-coated garden wire (3.5mm/0.14in wide) Wire cutters • Green florist tape • Twine

1. Cut out about 140 option 2 poppy leaves. Apply a small bead of glue to the bottom of one, then take another and stick the two together so they fan out very slightly. Turn the leaves over and apply a line of hot glue to the bottom leaf and attach a piece of thin florist wire, trimming it so it is 5cm (2in) long. Repeat with all the leaves so you have 70 leaf pairs. Make 18 yellow cherry blossom, 12 aster and 21 jasmine flowers for the wreath. Cut out and wire 8 green ranunculus leaves to add into the mix.

2. To make the base, use a circular object – such as a dinner plate about 27cm (10½in) in diameter. Cut your garden wire to the length of the circumference of the plate, allowing an excess of 10cm (4in). Shape the wire into a circle, using the plate as a guide, and overlap the ends then wrap them together tightly with green florist tape.

3. Split the flowers and foliage into two groups, so you know how many you have to work with for each half of the wreath.

4. Take two sets of leaves and, using florist tape, wrap them tightly to secure them to the wire base, positioning the leaves on either side of the wire. Once attached, spread the leaves apart slightly. (See page 26 for how to attach leaves to a stem.)

5. Take your paper flowers and, with a pair of pliers, bend the heads so they face upwards when against the base. Attach with florist tape, and cut any excess off the stems. Position the flowers so they are evenly spaced, adding in more as you go.

6. Once you have used all the flowers and leaves, arrange them so they are all facing forward. Carefully tie some twine to the back of the wreath to hang it from.

fuchsia

The fuchsia has quite a few different components, but once you have made up a few of the flowers this plant won't seem quite so complicated.

These look great displayed as little bunches of cut flowers but they also work well displayed in a plant pot in the same way as the Jasmine (page 112).

Real fuchsias come in so many different colours, but why not try them in pale pink or even a dark maroon colour?

you will need:

Fuchsia templates (page 133) • White, purple, dark purple and green paper • Pencil • Small sharp scissors • Florist wire (18-, 22- and 24-gauge) • Hot glue gun and glue sticks • Wooden skewer Bone folder • Green florist tape

instructions:

1. Photocopy 45 leaf templates, a mixture of large and small, onto your chosen paper, or photocopy all the templates onto some heavyweight paper and cut them out, then draw around them on your chosen paper. Cut out 9 of the outer petals, 27 of the inner petals, 9 of the long white stamen strips, 9 of the purple stamen strips following the marked lines on the template and 9 of the green strips.

    Wire the fuchsia leaves using the twisted wire technique (see page 47). Set aside.

    Using an 18-gauge wire, curl the long white stamens at one end of the strip, then repeat with the 9 purple stamens.

2. To make one flower, using a small amount of hot glue, attach one white and purple stamen to the end of a 22-gauge wire, making sure the white stamen is longer and in the middle of the purple one.

3. Next, using a skewer, curl 3 small inner petals lengthways (see page 40). Using some hot glue, stick these inner petals to the wire around the flower stamens, overlapping them slightly and evenly spacing them.

4. Take the larger white outer petals and using a bone folder or the back of a scissor blade, gently curl the petals upwards (see page 71).

5. Fold over the small tab on the white petals and apply a small amount of glue, then stick the tab to the opposite side to create a cone shape ensuring the petals are curled outwards. Cut off the very tip of the pointed cone to allow space for the wire stem to pass through.

6. Thread the wire stem through the hole in the white outer petals. Apply a small amount of glue to the purple inner petals near to the stem then slide the white outer petal upwards against the glue. Hold in place until the glue is set.

7. Take a green strip of paper and curl the whole length around an 18-gauge wire as tightly as possible, applying a tiny bead of glue at the end to secure it in place. Slide the small paper spiral off the wire and thread it onto the wire flower stem. Just before you reach the top, apply a small amount of glue around the base of the white petal and push the green spiral onto the end of the white outer petals. Hold the spiral in place whilst the glue dries.

8. Bend the flower stem over to one side and attach 5 leaves (see page 26), then repeat these steps for all the remaining pieces to make 9 flower stems in total.

9. Group 3 flower stems together and secure them using florist tape (see page 26). Repeat for all the remaining flowers to make 3 stems in total.

templates

ranunculus

flower

(note: this template is shown at 50%. To create the flower at the size shown on page 51 double the size of this template before you cut it out.)

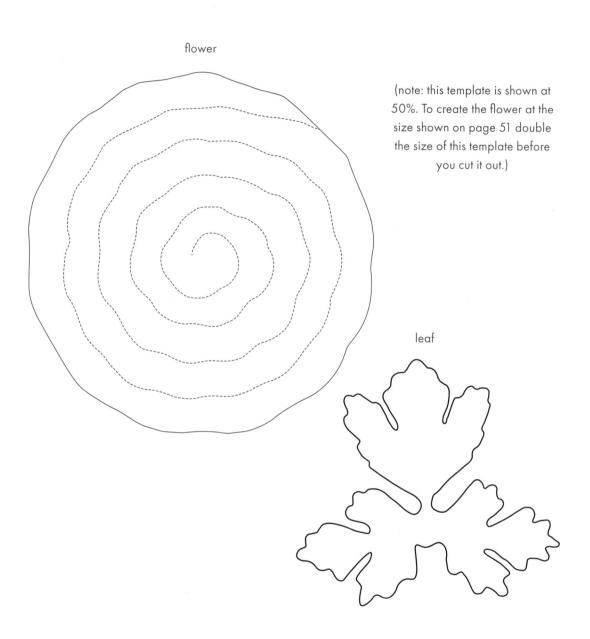

leaf

poppy

fringed stamen strip

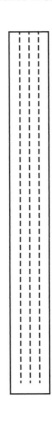

stamen star strips
(cut along the
dotted lines)

leaf option 1

petal

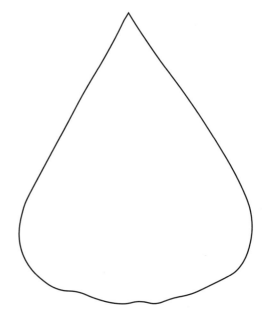

leaf option 2

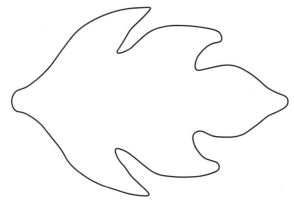

hellebore

small leaf

large leaf

petal

outer stamen
fringe

inner
stamen
fringe

chrysanthemum

medium
inner petal

central
petal strip

inner circle

outer petal

small
inner petal

leaf

131   templates

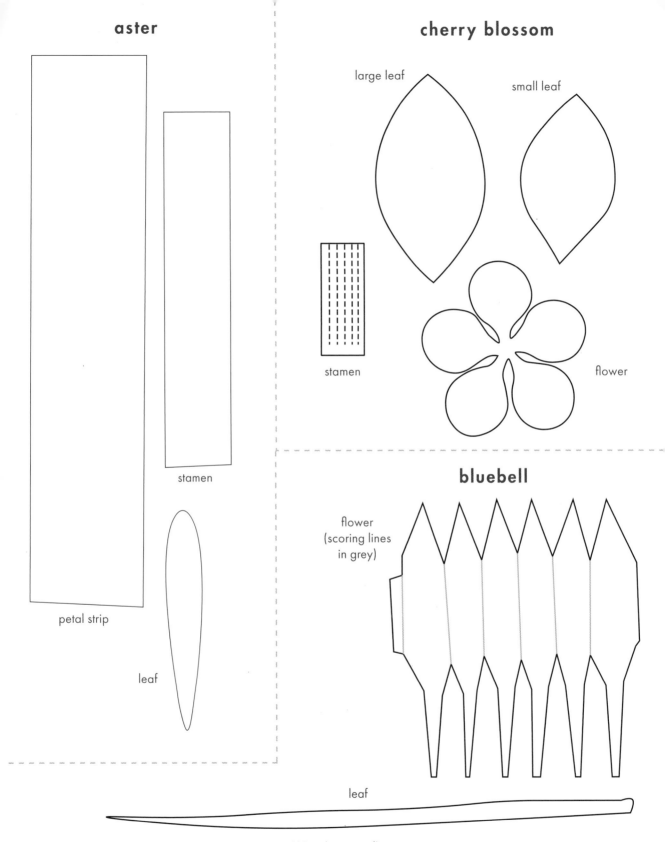

aster

petal strip

stamen

leaf

cherry blossom

large leaf

small leaf

stamen

flower

bluebell

flower
(scoring lines
in grey)

leaf

Fuchsia

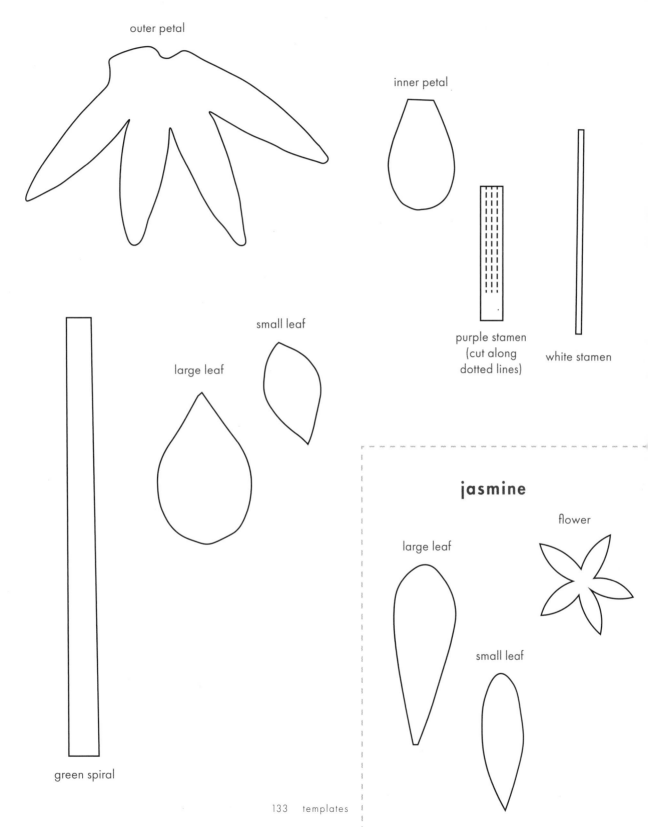

outer petal

inner petal

purple stamen
(cut along
dotted lines)

white stamen

small leaf

large leaf

green spiral

jasmine

large leaf

flower

small leaf

peony

large 4-petal

main leaf

large 5-petal

single petal

bud petal

bud calyx

peony cont.

stamen

inner petal

rose

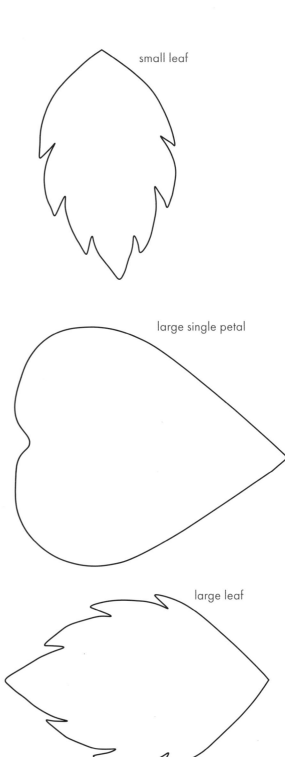

small leaf

large single petal

large leaf

large 5 petal

small 4 petal

small 3 petal

single single petal

rose cont.

large 4 petal

large 3 petal

resources

Colour Plan Papers:
www.gfsmith.com

James Cropper Paper Mills:
www.papermilldirect.co.uk

Daler Rowney Murano and Canford papers:
www.pullingers.com

www.saa.co.uk

Florist wire & Tape
www.thecraftcompany.co.uk

General craft supplies
www.hobbycraft.co.uk for glue gun, pliers,
craft mat and craft knife

www.paperchase.co.uk for washi tape and
decorative papers

www.wickes.co.uk for garden wire and wire cutters

index

An Hachette UK Company
www.hachette.co.uk

First published in Great Britain in 2019 by
Kyle Books, an imprint of Kyle Cathie Ltd
Carmelite House
50 Victoria Embankment
London EC4Y 0DZ
www.kylebooks.co.uk

ISBN: 978 0857 835 376

Text copyright 2019 © Suzi McLaughlin
Design and layout copyright 2019 © Kyle Books
Photography copyright 2019 © Anna Batchelor

Distributed in the US by Hachette Book Group, 1290
Avenue of the Americas, 4th and 5th Floors, New York,
NY 10104

Distributed in Canada by Canadian Manda Group,
664 Annette St., Toronto, Ontario, Canada M6S 2C8

Publisher: Joanna Copestick
Editor: Hannah Coughlin
Design: Hart Studio
Photography: Anna Batchelor
Styling: Tamineh Dhondy
Production: Lisa Pinnell

A Cataloguing in Publication record for this title is
available from the British Library

Printed and bound in China

10 9 8 7 6 5 4 3 2 1

acknowledgements

My fiancé Steve for always encouraging me to
do what I love and for always supporting my
creative journey.

To my mum and dad for teaching me the importance
of hard work and determination.

Thank you to Bev and Becky for all of your time
and help.

To Judith, Hannah and the team at Kyle Books for
approaching me to do this book. It has always
been a dream of mine.

Anna & Tam for your beautiful photography
and styling, and Abi for your wonderful design.

Thank you all.